LIBERATED

A World War II Memoir
of
Lt. Harlan E. Highfield

by
W. C. Highfield

In memory of my father,

Harlan E. Highfield, Sr.

(Oct. 21, 1915 – Feb. 7, 1995)

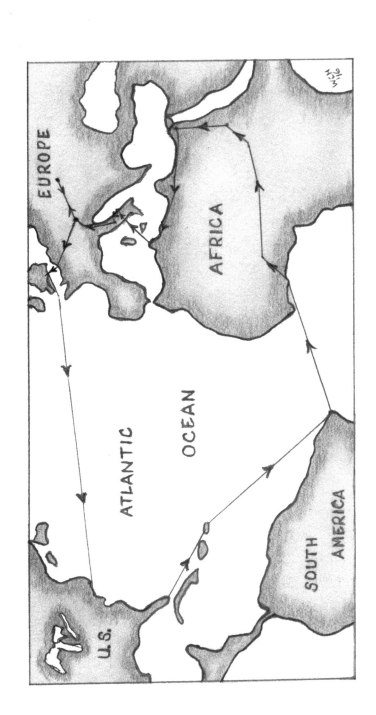

Introduction

My father's experiences during World War II can certainly be described as noteworthy. Hence, the purpose of this book is to chronologically detail his involvement in the conflict beginning with the December 7, 1941 Japanese attack on Pearl Harbor. A brief review of his early life, and a summary of his later interests and accomplishments will act as bookends around the war years.

As has been the case with many WWII veterans, my father was somewhat reluctant to volunteer remembrances of his war experiences. However, if requests were made, he would agreeably relate specific information. It remains a regret of mine to have not asked him more questions. But in retrospect, I find comfort in knowing that it was therefore not necessary for him to repeatedly relive a very traumatic time in his life. As did many others, he wanted to turn the page on what was an incredibly distressing period.

A memoir can be written from either an autobiographical or a biographical perspective. This book will consist of both. The format will be in a two-part presentation. In the font you are now reading will be my personal remembrances of conversations or supplemental research information. In italics will be my father's conversational style that I have transferred from the records he left behind, as in:

Things were rough all over.

Much of the chapter, "Early Years," comes from a letter he wrote to my son (his grandson), Bryan C. Highfield, in 1988. Although Bryan was only three at the time, he wanted to document parts of his life for future review.

In contrast, most of his notes regarding wartime are either individual words or short phrases—only occasional complete sentences. For ease of reading, I have added a minimum of additional words that are necessary to create his narrative. It has been my intent to accurately convey his personality and his manner of speech. Virtually all of the detailed descriptions are his entirely. His verbatim use of colloquial expressions of the time will also appear. These include the terms "Jerry" for German adversaries, "Arabs" for locals in North Africa, "Aussies," and other commonly used jargon.

All war is hell. But, World War II was the deadliest military conflict in history. It is estimated that the total dead from all countries ranged from 50 to 80 million. Approximately 21 to 25 million of the world's military forces perished. That number includes about 5 million in captivity. The United States sustained over 400,000 military casualties. These figures do not include the vast number of wounded, and millions upon millions more who were affected by the war.

In view of these staggering statistics, there comes a time to remember and note the individual sacrifices our servicemen and women made in defense of the freedom we enjoy today. This is one person's story.

Early Years

Harlan Edward Highfield was born in Pennsville, New Jersey on October 21, 1915. He was the first child of Clarence Junius Highfield and Emily Baynard Highfield.

There are no memories of Pennsville. At that time, my father worked in a munitions plant and my mother was an elementary school teacher. When I was four or five, we moved to a fairly large farmhouse on the Lancaster Pike near Hockessin, Delaware where we became farmers to help my grandparents. Later, my father got into the road and lane repair business.

My mother taught me first grade at home, since I was not in particularly good health. Then I walked to a one-room school for five years. Sometimes in winter my father took me to school on horseback when the snow was too deep across the fields or on the roads.

Growing up, I attended Red Clay Creek Presbyterian Church where I was active in Boy Scouts, both as a Scout and later an Assistant Scout Master.

Before I was 18, I worked for a neighboring farmer for a few cents a day during the seasons of strawberries, potatoes, shucking wheat, and moving hay. At age 18, my father couldn't stop me from getting my driver's license. I drove a dump truck for his business for a short time after high school and in the summers during college.

At Alexis I. DuPont High School in Wilmington, I was enrolled in the college prep course. I didn't work very hard so I failed and repeated the twelfth grade. This was a tough lesson, but dropping out was not a consideration. During my extra year, my grades improved and I was accepted at Bowling Green State University in Ohio where I earned a bachelor's degree, majoring in English and biology. I also had minors in sociology and physical education.

My father always displayed modesty in regard to his accomplishments—never seeking attention or praise. Therefore, I will enumerate his other avocations during college (where he was nicknamed "Hal"), as he would likely gloss over this impressive list:

- Member of the Commoners (social and service fraternity)
- Secretary/Treasurer of Areopagus (literary fraternity)
- Editor of the yearbook (Senior year)
- Member of the Board of Publications

- Member of Pi Kappa Delta (oratory and public speaking fraternity)
- Three-year member of the Intercollegiate Debate Team
- Member of Philosophy Club
- Member of the Inter-fraternity Council

It was during Harlan's college years that his parents moved from the farm on Lancaster Pike to Bear, Delaware, about ten miles southwest of Wilmington. They purchased a large rural farm and leased out the farming activities. In later years, they sold off smaller lots of the farm for houses, which fronted Route 7.

Harlan continues:

In high school I played first-string baseball and football, and at Bowling Green I played a year of freshman football. On the football team I was relegated to the second string. Each week, we were the ones that learned the plays of the upcoming opponent, and practiced them against the varsity. I weighed about 115 pounds. My junior year of college the school built a baseball field and I played on the team as a catcher. However, I had limited batting skills against college pitching.

I also played fraternity league volleyball and basketball. I was in a boxing tournament and was eliminated in the semi-finals! I also got a little interested in fast-pitch softball and learned to play golf (not too well!).

After graduating from Bowling Green in the summer of 1939, I became a seventh and eighth grade General Science teacher at Richardson Park Elementary School just outside of Wilmington. The fact that I had played high school sports and a year of college baseball made the difference with the other three or four candidates. I had previously coached youth baseball, and was interested in coaching at the school.

My first year of coaching baseball at Richardson Park, our team won 3 games and lost 4. It was the only losing record in a season of coaching baseball I ever had—before or after!

There was a pretty, young, third grade teacher on the second floor, and I took her home from a few P.T.A. meetings. Our first real date was to see the Wilmington Blue Rocks professional baseball team play. Her name was Beulah Papperman.

Harlan, age 24, Summer 1940, Mgr. Bear Cubs

Richardson Park Jr. High Baseball Team,
Spring 1941

1941

In the fall of 1941, Harlan turned twenty-six and was in his third year of teaching and coaching at Richardson Park School. On the afternoon of Sunday, December 7, 1941, his mother accompanied him to a Wilmington Clippers (American Football Association) professional football game. Played at one-year-old Wilmington Park, located at East 30th Street and the newly-opened Governor Printz Boulevard, it was an exhibition game against the Richmond Arrows of the South Atlantic (Dixie) League. The meeting was between two teams with winning records in neighboring leagues. The day's headline in the sports section of The Wilmington Sunday Morning Star proclaimed, "Big Crowd Expected to See Clippers in Exhibition Game Today." Early in the game it was announced over the loud speakers that the Japanese had attacked Pearl Harbor in Hawaii. All military troops were instructed to return immediately to their posts.

Six days later, on Saturday, December 13, Harlan enlisted in the U.S. Army Air Corps (which would become the U.S. Air Force in 1947). He had not been drafted in the national draft that had begun in 1940, which was the first peacetime draft in U.S. history. Although Harlan had no experience whatsoever with flying, it was his noted desire, in his words, to *"get home not wounded."* His rationale was that a fighter pilot would return from the war in one piece or not at all. It was highly unlikely his wish would take several ironic twists.

The day after Christmas, Harlan left for pilot training. His first stop was Shaw Field in Sumter, South Carolina.

1942

The cover photo shows Harlan with his first training airplane, a Stearman PT-13, at Shaw Field. In the 1930s and 40s, many different models of this biplane were the standard basic trainer for pilots in the U. S. Army and Navy. Over 10,000 were built in the United States during that time frame. The Royal Canadian Air Force referred to them as Kaydets during World War II.

After the war, a large number of these rugged airplanes were sold by the military and have since been used for transport, agricultural flying, airshows, and much more. In all cases of its history, Stearmans were the first choice for maneuverability and aerobatic performance.

Flying activities at Shaw Field had only begun on October 22, 1941, and the first class of potential pilots commenced their training on December 15—eight days after the Pearl Harbor attack. Arriving during the last few days of December, Harlan was in one of the earliest training classes at Shaw.

In researching this book, it became apparent that earning one's pilot's wings was no easy feat. Records show that a great number of cadets "washed out"—the term for failing to meet the required criteria for advancing in training. One prerequisite was having adequate visual depth perception. A test for that aptitude was to look into a dark tunnel and pull strings that were connected to two white stakes until the stakes were aligned directly next to each other. As mentioned previously, my father was never one to boast. But on several occasions, I specifically remember him commenting on his ability to be consistently accurate in passing that particular test.

Harlan graduated from primary training on March 12, 1942, and was assigned to Spence Field in Moultrie, Georgia. At Spence his training plane was the AT-6 Texan, which was commonly known as "the pilot maker" because of its important role in preparing pilots for combat. In all, over 15,000 of the planes were built before, during, and after the war. The AT-6 was one of the final aircraft used by training pilots during WWII before stepping up to a true fighter plane. In the early stages of the war, the required flight hours for combat pilots earning their wings had been reduced to just 200 during a shortened training period of seven months. Of those hours, 75 were logged in the AT-6. Conversely, cadets in the infantry completed their basic training in a mere three months.

AT-6 Texan on display at Page Field,
Fort Myers, Fla., 2016

Advanced training was completed at Spence on August 5, and Harlan was awarded his pilot's wings. He returned home to Wilmington, Delaware for a brief leave, as he had done several times during his training. However, on this particular visit he married the "pretty, young, third grade teacher," Beulah Papperman. The ceremony on Sunday, August 9, 1942 was held in the backyard of her parents' home on West 23rd Street in Wilmington.

The following announcement appeared in the next day's Wilmington newspaper:

"Announcement has been made by Mr. and Mrs. Charles W. Papperman of this city of the marriage of their daughter, Miss Beulah W. Papperman, to Lieut. Harlan E. Highfield, U.S. Army Air Corps, son of Mr. and Mrs. C. J. Highfield of Bear.

The wedding ceremony was performed on Sunday afternoon at the home of the bride's parents by the Rev. Dr. Willard Glenn Purdy, pastor of First and Central Presbyterian Church.

Mr. Papperman gave his daughter in marriage. Her only attendant was her sister, Mrs. A. C. Tweed, Jr. Mr. Wilfred H. Miller, Jr., of Richardson Park was best man.

A small reception for members of the immediate families and a few intimate friends followed the ceremony.

The bride is a graduate of the Women's College, University of Delaware, and is a teacher at Richardson Park School.

Lieutenant Highfield received his wings last Wednesday from the Army advanced flying school at Spence Field, Moultrie, Ga. He is now stationed at Bedford, Mass. He is a graduate of the Bowling Green State University of Bowling Green, O.

Following the reception, Lieutenant and Mrs. Highfield left on a wedding trip."

Beulah W. Papperman and Lt. Harlan E.
Highfield, wedding portrait, August 9, 1942

After the wedding, the newlyweds drove to Hartford, Connecticut where Harlan had been assigned for his initial training in the Curtiss P-40 Warhawk fighter plane. Warhawk was the U.S. nickname for the aircraft, while the British referred to that model as either Tomahawk or Kittyhawk. The next month or so served as the couple's honeymoon while Harlan participated in P-40 training at Rentschler Field, three miles east of Hartford.

The P-40 was first produced in 1938 and was originally conceived as a pursuit aircraft. It was very agile at low and medium altitudes, but suffered due to lack of power at higher altitudes. At medium and high speeds it was one of the tightest early monoplane designs of the war. Although the P-40 lacked some of the aeronautical innovations of the time, it had a strong structure that enabled the plane to pull high G turns.

The P-40 was the only fighter aircraft available when the U.S. entered WWII. However, it was the most controversial fighter to serve in quantity during the war. It was praised and criticized. Its shortcomings were compensated for by its ease of handling and control, in addition to its sturdiness and durability. P-40s could withstand a considerable amount of punishment. All told, well over 13,000 were built. It was the third most produced fighter of the war, after the P-51 Mustang and the P-47 Thunderbolt.

The P-40s' lack of a two-speed supercharger made it inferior to German fighters such as the Messerschmitt BF-109 or the Focke-Wulf FW-190 in high-altitude combat. However, the P-40's use in the North Africa Campaign, and elsewhere, was primarily for ground attack or bomber support—so its lack of performance at higher altitudes was not as important.

Lt. Highfield and P-40, Rentschler Field, Hartford, Conn., Sept. 1942

Beulah and Harlan on honeymoon,
Hartford, Conn., Sept. 1942

Harlan and Beulah's honeymoon ended when he was assigned to the 79th Fighter Group and was sent to gunnery school at Dale Mabry Field, just west of Tallahassee, Florida. After the war, Dale Mabry was closed, and in the early 1960s became the campus of Tallahassee Community College. Some of the former runways are used for parking at the school.

There were two distinct versions of gunnery training – flexible and fixed. Flexible gunnery training was for use in bombers (i.e., waist gunner, rear gunner). This type of firing was of a dynamic nature where the operator could rotate the machine gun in various directions. With fixed gunnery, the machine guns were located within the wings of fighter planes. P-40s were equipped with six .50 caliber machine guns—three on each wing.

The 79th Fighter Group consisted of approximately ninety pilots who were divided into three squadrons, the 85th, 86th, and 87th. Harlan (nicknamed "Hife") was a member of the 87th Fighter Squadron. After completing gunnery school, the group began their circuitous journey to the ongoing combat in North Africa. It was during this period that Harlan turned twenty-seven.

A transport flight southward from Miami, via Puerto Rico, to Natal, Brazil put the pilots of the three squadrons at the closest geographical point in South America to the western coast of Central Africa.

87th Fighter Squadron, Dale Mabry Field,
Tallahassee, Fla.,
Lt. Highfield, second row from top, second from right

Miami, Fla., Oct. 1942, Lt. Highfield on left

Preparing for flight to Brazil, Oct. 23, 1942,
Lt. Highfield kneeling, second from left

The aircraft used for the group's flight across the Atlantic was a Boeing 314 Clipper. Manufactured from 1938-41, only twelve of the "Flying Boats," as they were called, were ever produced. It was a civilian plane primarily used by Pan American Airlines and the British Overseas Air Corporation. Designed of massive proportions, the Clipper was intended for "one-class" luxury air travel, which was necessary due to the long duration of trans-oceanic flights. The Clipper fleet was pressed into military duty during WWII, and the Flying Boats were used for transporting personnel and equipment to the North Africa, European, and Pacific Theaters. Although the Clippers were designated the C-98 for military purposes, they continued to be flown by their experienced Pan Am civilian crews.

In late October 1942, the pilots of the 79th Fighter Group touched down in the British colony of Gold Coast, which would become the independent nation of Ghana in 1957. Based near the capital of Accra, the group had an extended four-week layover while their P-40s were assembled. The fighters lacked the long-range capability of a trans-oceanic flight, which required the components of the planes to be ferried across the Atlantic. His notes from this time:

4 weeks   sleeping until noon
swimming in afternoon   some test flying

coconuts   pineapple
(never liked coconuts or pineapple before)
river trip   Slavery 1562
forts   castles   tribal law
Education   12 years English (4 yrs. free)
tin cans   football   clothing
names—day of week   "Chop-chop"
"dash"   playing poker
book – pocketbook – bookends – tusk

The last four terms are various gifts Harlan sent back to Beulah while he was stationed in Gold Coast. Other items obtained there, he kept with him as his tour progressed. I am still in possession of several of these mementos mentioned, in addition to an ivory-handled letter opener with embossed leather sheath, and a carved wooden picture frame with the wording, "Africa 1942" and "Gold Coast." There is also a carved elephant at the bottom of the frame. The craftsmanship is remarkable.

Natal, Brazil, October 1942,
Lt. Highfield on left

Lt. Highfield in front of barracks
in Gold Coast, Africa

In early November, the 79th Fighter Group flew east to Lagos, Nigeria aboard a C-47 Skytrain. The C-47, known as the "Gooney Bird," was a military transport aircraft that was developed from the Douglas DC-3 civilian airliner. It was used extensively by the Allies during World War II, and remains in front line service with various military operators to the present day.

From Lagos, the three squadrons of the 79th began their lengthy journey across the continent of Africa in their newly-assembled, single-seat P-40s. The total distance flown was well over 3,500 miles—farther than from New York to Los Angeles. Harlan's notes indicate fueling stopovers at Kano, Nigeria; Ft. Lamy, Chad (then-French Equatorial Africa); and El Fasher, Sudan on the eastward trip to Khartoum, Sudan. From Khartoum, the flight path turned north with stops at Umm Nabari, Sudan and Luxor, Egypt. Harlan noted that the surrounding area of Luxor contains numerous ruins of ancient monuments, temples, and tombs on both sides of the Nile River.

On November 18, 1942, the group arrived at Kasfareet Airfield, near the city of Suez, which is 100 miles east of Cairo, Egypt. The following are Harlan's recollections as his fighter group progressed westward toward the front lines in Libya to face the enemy forces of Germany and Italy:

We spent one night in Cairo. Saw the Sphinx and crawled up in into one of the Pyramids. Took in a night club.

I nearly hit the cliffs taking off. Arrived in the desert in time for Christmas 1942—real nice—had Spam for dinner. Heard over the radio that all service men had turkey.

Saw a mirage—they are real.

Carriage ride in Alexandria, Egypt,
Lt. Highfield, front right

Cairo, Egypt, Dec. 1942,
Lt. Highfield on right – Sphinx and pyramid in background

1943

In a couple of sand storms—stayed in tent for three days—had to use a gasmask to go after food. The tents were dispersed—had to use pistol for signal if lost. I won all the tosses and never had to go for chow.

Fooled around with barrage balloons over Tobruk, Libya. The most completely wrecked town you can picture—ships in harbor.

Had a party with Aussies and had some stuff that tasted like Scotch they brought over in a couple of five-gallon cans. After that, we stuck to Purple Passion or Pale Passion. Purple was powdered grape juice, gin, and some water. With Pale, the grape juice was replaced with powdered lemon juice. All was well until some thoughtless fellow used enough lemon powder for five gallons, with only a gallon of gin and water. A couple of the guys got real sick. General wants to see me?

The North Africa Campaign had begun on June 10, 1940. It pitted the combined Allied forces of Britain, Australia, New Zealand, the Republic of South Africa, and Poland against the Axis military of Germany and Italy (which had just entered the war). Many of these countries on both sides had colonial interests at stake in Africa dating back to the late 1800s. Also, control of North Africa meant control of the southern portion of the Mediterranean Sea and access to the oil-rich Middle East. It should be noted that this portion of WWII began a year and a half before the United States entered the war after the Pearl Harbor attack – and almost two full years before U.S. forces began direct military assistance to the Allies in North Africa.

The Axis forces were commanded by German Field Marshall Erwin Rommel, who became known as The Desert Fox. He was a skilled military strategist whose success in North Africa was limited only by lack of fuel and supplies. British Lieutenant-General Bernard Montgomery led the Allies in the back-and-forth pushing match in the desert that lasted three years. On the ground, tank and artillery units played a big role for both sides. The bulk of all combat took place on an east/west strip of the North African coast that ran some 2,500 miles wide (from Cairo to Casablanca) and roughly 100 miles in depth—bordered on the north by the Mediterranean Sea.

Harlan's comments about the extreme damage he witnessed in the port city of Tobruk stem from two sieges that took place in the preceding years of the war. The first was a British attack that resulted in an Italian defeat and a change in control of the port. The second, and more devastating, siege lasted 241 days as Allied forces fiercely defended the port from relentless Axis attack. Tobruk was frequently bombarded by artillery from the land and bomber attacks from the air. Port cities along the Mediterranean coast were vital for access to supplies and reinforcements.

In early 1943, the 79th Fighter Group advanced westward through Libya along the coast of the Mediterranean, passing through the port cities of Bengasi (now Benghazi) and Tripoli. On March 13, 1943, the 79th transferred from Landing Ground 150 in Libya to Causeway Landing Ground in Tunisia.

The following day, the 85th Squadron and 87th Squadron, including Harlan, flew their first combat mission as twelve P-40s escorted eleven B-25 bombers on a mission against the Mareth Line.

The Mareth Line was a system of fortifications built by France in Southern Tunisia in 1939, prior to World War II. It was intended to defend against attacks from Libya, then a colony of Fascist Italy. However, the reverse happened after the German Afrika Korps and Italian 1st Army occupied Tunisia in late 1942.

The Axis forces of Germany and Italy used the line to defend against the advancing British Eighth Army (to which Harlan's 79th Fighter Group was attached). The line had been refurbished by the Axis with more than 62 miles of barbed wire, 100,000 anti-tank mines, and 70,000 anti-personnel mines. Bunkers had been reinforced with concrete, and were armed with anti-tank and anti-aircraft guns. After the Allies' successful Battle of the Mareth Line (March 19-27), Axis forces retreated northward in Tunisia toward the coast of the Mediterranean.

During a fifteen-day period, Harlan flew six bomber support and/or strafing missions.

His notes:

On the night of March 28, I got in a poker game and won a pretty big pot from the Major, who was the Commanding Officer. He promised me the next strafing mission.

The next day, on March 29, I was not scheduled to fly, so I left the line and went to the mess tent. A little while later a couple of other fellows came down. I had finished eating. Then came a Jeep looking for a pilot. Someone's plane wasn't revving up. Sand was always getting into everything. One of my messmates, a Captain, looks around and says, "Lieutenant, you have finished your banquet, and we are just starting. Don't you think it would be considerate of you to go?" Rank having its privileges, I go.

Flew over the corner of the Mediterranean—low down to avoid radio contact, and into the setting sun.

Jerry moving out in three tracks.

I pulled up over trees, dropped down and started shooting. Somebody shot back. Ground fire.

Instrument panel all red. I pull up to bail out, but no altitude, and I would have been scared to jump anyway.

Early in my flight training there had been some doubt as to my ultimate ability to land a plane. In fact, I held an unofficial record for height bounced off a runway in South Carolina.

Anyway, I fulfilled my fondest hopes—I made a perfect landing in the desert—no wheels. It was the last landing I made in a plane. With no room for improvement, it seemed like a good place to call a halt to this flying foolishness.

[The "no wheels" landing was intentional. During training, fighter pilots were specifically instructed **not** to use the landing gear if an emergency touchdown became necessary in the desert. The wheels of the plane making contact with the uneven terrain had a high probability of catching a low spot on the ground, causing the aircraft to flip over and kill the pilot. The no wheels landing was a maneuver that was taught, but never practiced in training.]

As soon as the plane stopped, I radioed the flight, telling them to expect me in a few days. The mountains were only a few miles away, and Jerry was on the run so fast that the 20 miles

I was behind his lines should soon shrink to nothing.

I was standing on the wing of the plane just a couple of feet above the ground having this chat with an Arab, when I caught a glimpse of a plane diving toward me. There were big red basketballs coming at me. They looked like golf balls when I shot 'em, but tracers used by Jerry looked a heck of a lot bigger. Then a feeling something like getting hit by a baseball bat all over at the same time happened, and I hit the ground. It seemed like about 1 hour and 27 minutes before he flew over me, though about 3-4 seconds would be more accurate.

I had been hit in the left arm and right leg. I got up and started to run. I remembered a gully I had crossed over just before landing. I got down in the grass, and the Messerschmitt circled back, shooting. My yellow Mae West in the green must have been right outstanding. [During WWII, Allied aircrew called their yellow, inflatable, vest-like life preserver jackets, Mae Wests. She was a well-known actress, singer, comedienne, and sex symbol—with a buxom figure.]

After the German fighter made a 3rd pass, I went back to the plane for the first aid kit. That trip was brief since the plane was now on fire and I figured there were over 100 gallons still in the fuel tank.

The left front pocket of my shirt that had been holding a pair of glasses and a pack of cigarettes had been shot off.

I went up a hill where there were Arabs. Wasn't sure of their sympathies. I got a ride from an Arab on his donkey to the next village and gave him my Bowling Green University class ring. Rode to another village—dogs of the Arabs—women. I was going into shock. Chills— tried to stop bleeding with a robe (flowing, not white or clean)—lice.

I was in bad shape. Got picked up by a German patrol and rode in the sidecar of a motorcycle to a German field hospital a few miles away. The medic who dressed my wounds with a rough manner was in a bad humor. He thought my unit had strafed his tent earlier in the day. We may have.

The next day I was dropped off at an Italian hospital in the town of Sfax where my wounds were dressed more skillfully—but rough and painfully. Later, I was placed on an Italian hospital ship enroute to Italy. Aboard the ship, a nun-nurse asked for my nearest of kin, so she could contact them. I gave her my wife's name and address.

The sequence of notifications making their way back to Beulah, regarding Harlan's condition and whereabouts, must have been lengthy and excruciatingly stressful. She was initially notified by the War Department that Harlan had been listed as Missing in Action. The next day, the following article appeared in the Wilmington newspaper:

Richardson Park Man Missing in Air Action

Lieutenant Harlan E. Highfield, 27-year-old Army fighter pilot and former member of the Richardson Park School faculty, has been reported missing in action since March 29.

The word was received from the War Department last night by his wife, the former Miss Beulah W. Papperman, who is also a Richardson Park teacher. She lives at 606 West Twenty-third Street.

It is presumed the action was in North Africa.

The pilot's parents, Mr. and Mrs. Clarence J. Highfield of Bear, and his wife are optimistic, hoping he was able to parachute to safety.

Lieutenant Highfield is a graduate of Bowling Green College, Ohio. He received his wings and commission at Spence Field, Moultrie, Ga.

Before entering the Army on Dec. 26, 1941, he coached basketball and baseball at the Richardson Park

School. He was a member of Red Clay Creek Presbyterian Church.

There appears to be a contradiction between the newspaper article reporting that the family was hoping he was able to parachute to safety, and the fact that Harlan had radioed to his base that he was safely on the ground. It's reasonable to assume there was not a perfectly accurate recording of all details.

After an unknown and no-doubt agonizing period of time, a Catholic priest from the Wilmington Parish visited Harlan's in-laws' home, where Beulah lived during the war. Neither the Highfield or Papperman family were Roman Catholic. The priest delivered a message sent from a diocese in Italy, letting Beulah know that Harlan was a Prisoner of War. The information Harlan had given to the nun-nurse on the Italian hospital ship as it crossed the Mediterranean Sea had eventually made its way back to Beulah in Wilmington.

Shortly thereafter, Beulah received a package of Harlan's belongings, which included the previously mentioned wooden picture frame. The items had been packed and sent home from the Army Air Corps Home Field located between Alexandria and Cairo, Egypt, when Harlan did not return from the mission.

Richardson Park Man Missing in Air Action

Lieut. Harlan E. Highfield

Lieutenant Highfield, 27-year-old Army fighter pilot and former member of the Richardson Park School faculty, has been reported missing in action since March 29.

This word was received from the War Department last night by his wife, the former Miss Beulah W. Papperman, who is also a Richardson Park teacher. She lives at 606 West Twenty-third Street.

It is presumed the action was in North Africa.

The pilot's parents, Mr. and Mrs. Clarence J. Highfield of Bear, and his wife are optimistic, hoping he was able to parachute to safety.

Lieutenant Highfield is a graduate of Bowling Green College, Ohio. He received his wings and commission at Spence Field, Moultrie, Ga.

Before entering the Army on Dec. 26, 1941, he coached basketball and baseball at the Richardson Park School. He was a member of Red Clay Creek Presbyterian Church.

Picture frame from Gold Coast, Africa

Carved bookends from Gold Coast, Africa

I still have an intriguing United States one-dollar bill that was included in the shipment. It has the signatures of twenty-one men's names on the front of the bill. At one end it is entitled, "Short Snorter Highfield." The cultivation and use of opium in Egypt dates from as early as circa 1300 B.C. One is left to assume that servicemen in the North Africa Campaign may have indulged in opium's recreational use due to its ready availability. Considering the life-threatening dangers that fighter pilots faced during the war, a temporary escape from that reality is certainly understandable.

There were several ironic circumstances that led to Harlan's wounding and capture. First, he was not scheduled to fly on the day of the fateful mission. As a result of another pilot's plane not starting, he was pressed into service. Also, although he was able to successfully crash-land his plane without injury, his subsequent wounding occurred while he was on the ground with his P-40 totally disabled.

In addition, when the Axis forces surrendered and/or evacuated Tunisia on May 13, 1943, they released all Allied prisoners in their control. It would have meant that had Harlan been captured without having been wounded, he would have been returned to Allied forces in roughly six weeks. Or, as he made a point of mentioning, he could have hidden out in the nearby mountainous terrain and been reunited with the advancing Allies in a matter of several days.

Harlan continues:

On the hospital ship to Naples, Italy, I saw Mount Vesuvius out of the porthole. It was very impressive at night.

I stayed in the hospital in Naples for three months (one month with dope) while I recovered from my wounds. I could still see Mount Vesuvius from the hospital.

Then I was put on a train that took me from Naples eastward across Italy to an Italian-controlled camp designated as P.G. 132. It was near the town of Foggia. Many POWs there, mostly British, had been wounded. There were escapes and there was jaundice. We were moved northward to another camp (P.G. 21) near Chieti, on the Italian coast of the Adriatic Sea. New camp not bad. There were several escapes from the new camp, and some of the escapees were shot.

It is from this camp that Harlan sent a postcard to Bill Wood, of Wilmington, who Harlan had coached in youth baseball prior to the war. The postcard is dated July 30, 1943, and contains the following:

May be a long time before you get this, but if you ever do, it will make a souvenir! Have been "in the bag" since March 29—three months of that in hospital, due to a bad strafing mission!

Am ok now an' raring to go.....Pretty soft life—
play ball, cards, read and sleep. Sure want to get
home.

In 2001, the recipient, Bill Wood, forwarded the postcard to the Highfield family with a thoughtful note. The following are excerpts:

"Enclosed is a postcard from your Dad which was sent to my home while I was in the service. No doubt it is an interesting piece of the Highfield family history. I met your dad when he coached my brother Ken at Richardson Park. Later he signed Bill Shirk, a pitcher, and me, a catcher, to play ball for his team at Bear. We signed for a hot dog and a coke at the Texas Weiner restaurant in Wilmington. This had to be the largest payoff for free agents at that time. We always had a lot of fun recalling that."

Camp P.G. 21 was a former convent used to hold Allied officers. Conditions were generally good, as was the case with most of the Italian-controlled camps. The variety of food supplied by the Italians, coupled with regular rations from the Red Cross, made for a superior diet compared to POW camps in Germany.

During the summer of 1943, Italy recognized the futile prospects of continuing to fight the larger and better equipped Allied forces who had captured Sicily and were on the verge of invading the Italian mainland. After a period of protracted negotiations, an armistice was announced on September 8, 1943. Italian forces put down their arms and, in most cases, returned to civilian life.

For Allied POWs held in Italy, a void was created when Italian guards deserted the camps. What followed was a highly controversial action taken by Allied military headquarters. An order was issued for all POWs to remain in prison camps and await Allied forces. But within several days, German forces arrived at P.G. 21 (and other camps in Italy), easily taking control and recapturing thousands of unarmed Allied POWs.

It seems this order could be evaluated in several different ways. First, Allied forces had yet to invade and secure a foothold on the peninsula of Italy. Thus, masses of escaping POWs (without weapons, for the most part) would have no line of friendly forces to reach. Plus, German military occupied many areas of the country, and it was unknown how Italian civilians would act in response to the armistice. However, it certainly provided a captive audience for the Germans.

Once again, there was an ironic outcome for Harlan, as the situation could have provided an opportunity for freedom from capture— although under dangerous circumstances.

His notes:

One of our Colonels ordered us to not attempt to escape or we would be court-marshalled.

From there we were loaded onto trucks westbound toward Scanno. It was during this trip that I underwent one of the two worst experiences while a POW. We were driven to a soccer field and ordered to unload. There was a period of several hours where we felt we might be destroyed to relieve the transport problem. There was what was referred to as a "round up" and a "fake shoot."

Eventually, we were loaded into boxcars and traveled by train northbound toward Germany. As we were climbing in elevation, the train made frequent slowdowns. During the trip we hacked through the floor of the boxcar. One of our guys crawled out at one of the stops and unlocked the door of the boxcar. It was nighttime. At the next slowdown, three of us jumped out of the door and went down a steep embankment. The train stopped. German guards started firing guns down toward us in bright moonlight. After only several minutes, we thought they could see us so we raised our hands and surrendered. After we climbed up the bank and looked back down to where we had been, there was nothing but darkness. They couldn't have seen us at all.

As the train ascended into the Alps near Switzerland and the Brenner Pass, the second of the worst experiences happened. Our train was stopped in a marshalling yard, and the entire depot came under a heavy bombing attack by *the Allies* [so-called, "friendly fire"]. *This was a very scary thing...*

Roughly 120,000 Americans were held, at some point, as POWs (or Kriegies as the Germans called them – it was short for Kriegsgefangenen, meaning prisoners of war) by Germany during World War II in nearly 100 different camps. As a signatory to the Geneva Conventions, and fearful of reprisals against German POWs held by the Allies, Germany generally adhered to the measures outlined for humane treatment of prisoners of war. Officers were usually treated somewhat better than enlisted servicemen. None of this was the case for POWs held by Japan, however, where approximately 40% of POWs died in captivity during the war.

The first camp in Germany where Harlan was held was Stalag VII-A (7-A) in Moosburg, not far from Munich. It was the largest of the German-controlled camps. His stay was short-lived, as he and other pilots were sent in boxcars north and west approximately 300 miles to Stalag Luft III in Sagan, Germany.

The camp was located 100 miles south-east of Berlin in what is now Poland. Stalag Luft III was one of six operated by the Luftwaffe (German Air Force) for downed Allied airmen. The large majority of the prisoners were British, but during the course of the war well over 6,000 American POWs spent time in the camp. Harlan's information card, which he retained and is in my possession, shows an intake date of October 15, 1943. Stalag Luft III would be his home for the next fifteen months.

Upon his arrival, Harlan was led by German guards into one of the barracks and directed to an empty bunk. After the guards left, a fellow POW came over and suggested that Harlan find another available bunk. He told him it was not a good idea to take that particular one. Said he wouldn't be getting much sleep, since the entrance to a partially completed escape tunnel was under the bunk.

Six days later Harlan turned twenty-eight.

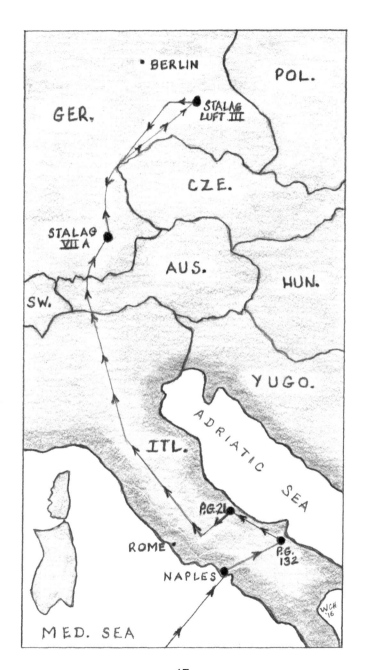

1944

The Luftwaffe took extensive measures to ensure their prisoners' confinement was secure. Around each of the three adjoining camps in the Stalag Luft III compound were two rows of nine-foot-high fencing, which provided an intimidating perimeter. The fences were covered in barbed wire and the rows sat about ten feet apart. The open space between the two rows was filled with an impenetrable mass of barbed wire.

Thirty to forty feet inside the double fence was a low, wooden one-rail fence. The space between the main outer fence and the guard rail was forbidden territory. Any Kriegie seen in this area would be shot. Even making mere contact with the wooden guard rail would subject the offender to the same fate.

The eight or nine guard towers that circled each of the camps were manned twenty-four hours a day by guards armed with machine guns. Each tower had a powerful spotlight that was in constant use during nighttime. Also at night, roving guards, accompanied by German police dogs, patrolled the interior of the camp.

Boredom and monotony were continuous negative forces that exerted themselves on the prisoners. Just as constant was the persistent effort by POWs to overcome those forces as best they could. Keeping a regular daily routine, along with social interaction with other prisoners, were several suggested remedies.

Two camp newspapers, one hand-printed and one typewritten, were issued each Sunday. Everything of possible interest was included in the papers—news from home, by way of letters; arrival of food parcel shipments; humor in cartoons; serious art; new book arrivals to the camp library; food recipes to be created with available ingredients; and poetry. Only single copies of the newspapers were produced, and they were posted on the walls of the newsroom (located in the theater building). These publications were eagerly anticipated and they contributed to improving overall morale.

In an attempt to counter feelings of futility and helplessness, a number of activities were established within the camp community. Classroom courses were offered by qualified POWs, and libraries were created. Participation in sporting events was encouraged, and many were carried out with the help of equipment provided by the YMCA. Boxing matches, track meets, along with football and baseball games were very popular. Wagering on these various events was widespread. Army-rationed chocolate bars and cigarettes were often the payoff for winning bets. Also, camp theaters produced plays—mostly comedies.

The POWs' most common physical exercise was known as "walking the perimeter." This meant following the wooden guard rail completely around the camp, which was a distance of three-quarters of a mile for the circuit. Many Kriegies regularly walked the perimeter at least once a day in an effort to maintain a suitable level of fitness.

Escape was a driving force for some, but not all, POWs. The majority were committed to live out the war and wait for liberation. In practically all cases, those who had been held the longest and who were directly involved in tunnel-digging were on the seniority list when it came to attempted escape.

Harlan has noted that tunnels were being dug all over the large camp, although he was not a participant. The Germans were on constant high alert to search out and discover any digging activity. Guards, referred to as "ferrets," would frequently crawl under the raised barracks in shallow tunnels of their own, looking for signs of POW tunnel construction. Eavesdropping on prisoner conversations from beneath the shoddily constructed buildings was also common.

The war's most famous escape attempt was what became known as The Great Escape, as depicted in the 1963 Hollywood movie of the same name. It was in Stalag Luft III where this event took place on the night of March 24-25, 1944. A total of 76 POWs, mostly British, managed to escape. Within several days, all but three were re-captured. The escape so angered Hitler that he ordered 50 of them to be shot.

There are several myths that surround the movie and prisoner escape in general. There was no specific policy that it was the duty of POWs to make an attempt to escape from enemy captivity. It is estimated that approximately two-thirds of prisoners had no interest in the activity. When they were shot down, Allied airmen were indeed expected to avoid being captured, but once they were in the hands of the enemy, there was no formal expectation that they should try to escape.

Although the movie depicts the weather conditions to appear ideal, the reality was that the region was still in the throes of its harshest winter in thirty years. Not only were temperatures near zero, most of the escapees were ill-prepared for the conditions due to the lightweight nature of their uniforms. Many were airmen who had been shot down in the warmer climate of North Africa.

Also, the movie implies that a mass escape attempt was unique. In fact, nearly a dozen Allied escapes of large numbers had occurred before The Great Escape. In practically all cases, they were carried out by British servicemen.

For American officers, there exists what is known as the Code of Conduct. It is an ethical guide to proper duty of a POW that is considered somewhat ambiguous and is broadly interpreted. Much of the Code deals with the responsibilities of the officer if he or she is subject to interrogation by the enemy. After reading an essay on the Code in the U. S. Naval Institute publication, "Proceedings," in 1987, Harlan wrote a letter to the author. It contained the following excerpts:

Hello Jim,

My recollections in this area are all: '... name, rank, and serial number.' I believe that my first contact was from our squadron commander in a tent in the African desert. I would guess that it was there I first heard, also, of '...try to escape.' I can't recall hearing any of this in flying school or at training bases in the United States or West Africa, but it is possible, because I really had little interest in those sessions!

There was very little, if any, conversation on the Code in the two years spent in POW camps.

I was asked no questions from the time I was turned over to the field hospital near Sfax, Tunisia, or on the Italian hospital ship. I gave a nun-nurse my wife's name and address on the ship, but nothing more. Nor were there any questions in the hospital near Naples, Italy, or in the two camps afterward in Italy. At the first camp in Germany (VII-A) I was interrogated. They were satisfied with an identification-type photo and with 'name, rank, and serial number.' I have the card with the above on it, photo and all. Its purpose was more to keep track of POWs, rather than to gather information.

From the POWs I knew (or heard!), my experience was much the same as the majority. A few had, I expect, more involvement with the Code.

On May 2, 1944, additional personal information was added to Harlan's information card. With the help of translation, the following was recorded:

Build: Lean   Height: 5'9"
Age: 28.7   Face: Oval
Eyes: Blue   Hair: Average Blonde
Beard: None   Nose: Straight Wide
Shape of Head: Oval   Teeth: Good –
Upper Right Side Tooth Missing

It should be noted that at the top of the information card both Stalag Luft III and Oflag Luft III are listed. Oflag was the portion of the larger camp that was designated for captured officers.

| 1 | 2 | 3 | 4 | 5 | 6 | 7 | 8 | 9 | 10 | 11 | 12 | 13 | 14 | 15 | 16 | 17 | 18 | 19 | 20 | 21 | 22 | 23 | 24 | 25 |

Personalkarte I: Personelle Angaben

Kriegsgefangenen-Stammlager: **Stalag Luft 3**

Beschriftung der Erkennungsmarke

Nr. *1744*

Lager O F L A G. L U F T. 8

Name: *HIGHFIELD*	Staatsangehörigkeit: **U.S.A.**
Vorname: *Harlan*	Dienstgrad: *2. Lt.*
Geburtstag und -ort: *11.10.15 Pennville, N.J.*	Truppenteil: *USAAF* Kom. usw.:
Religion: *keine*	Zivilberuf: *Lehrer* Berufs-Gr.:
Vorname des Vaters:	Matrikel Nr. (Stammrolle des Heimatstaates): *0-791705*
Familienname der Mutter:	Gefangennahme (Ort und Datum): *19.3.43 Nordafrika*
	Ob gesund, krank, verwundet eingeliefert:

Lichtbild

Nähere Personalbeschreibung

Besondere Kennzeichen:

Grösse	Haarfarbe
1.76	*m.blond*

Fingerabdruck des rechten Zeigefingers

Name und Anschrift der zu benachrichtigenden Person in der Heimat des Kriegsgefangenen

Mrs. Harlan E. Highfield (Frau)
606 W. 23rd St.
Wilmington,
Delaware

Des Kriegsgefangenen

54

Beschriftung der Erkennungsmarke Nr. ▦▦▦ Lager: ▦▦▦ Name:

Bemerkungen:

Personalbeschreibung

Figur:	schlank
Größe:	1,76
Alter:	28 J.
Gesicht:	oval
Haare:	dunkelblond
Bart:	klein
Augen:	graue braun
Nase:	
Gewicht:	
Schädelform:	oval
Gesichtsfarbe:	unv. gelb
Gebiß:	gut, oilig, unter Lücke
Besondere Merkmale:	
Deutsche Sprachkenntnisse:	

Der Kgf. wurde am *4.5.44* im Oflag ▦▦▦
nach Art. 70 Kgf.-Abk. v. 1929 der gem. Ärztekommission vorgestellt.
Seine Heimkehrberechtigung wurde verneint — bejaht.
Er ist der nächsten Sammelstelle vorzustellen.
Eingezogen i. d. Bfundstelle b. *Oflag Kgf 43 Lager*
.... *Lazarettaufnahme im Ort*
am *4.5.44* unt. lfd. Nr. *13*
_____

Food, or lack thereof, was a major issue for POWs. Germany had difficulties enough feeding its own people. Feeding POWs was well down on the list of priorities. The German POW rations were insufficient to sustain health, and failed to meet the requirements of the Geneva Conventions. Had the International Red Cross not shipped food parcels to Allied POW camps, serious malnutrition would have been pervasive. The wartime rail service in Germany was inconsistent for delivery of Red Cross rations, as well as frequent instances of poaching by camp guards. Sometimes Red Cross parcels were withheld intentionally as a form of punishment.

Bread was the main event in the camp diet. The heavy, black, five-pound loaves consisted of a soggy mixture of unknown ingredients, with a distinctive sour taste. POWs had to develop a taste for it. However, hunger in general and occasional toasting on room stoves, when fuel was available, helped overcome the bread's offensiveness. Daily rations of potatoes were the other main staple of an otherwise inadequate and unbalanced diet.

On a Veterans Administration form that Harlan completed in 1983, he noted the following under the heading, "Adequacy of Diet During Captivity:"

Water: Adequate   Broth: Inadequate
Bread: Adequate   Soup, with pieces of
fish, meat, or poultry: Inadequate
Rice: None   Legumes: Inadequate
Potatoes: Adequate   Meat: Inadequate
Dairy Products: Inadequate   Nuts: None
Fish: None   Fruits: None
Vegetables: Inadequate   Cereals: None

In an attempt to overcome the daily monotony of the repetitive diet, creativity became a hallmark of cooking. Various items from Red Cross parcels were used to experiment with what was hoped to be more appetizing concoctions. Most of the POWs had little or no cooking experience. But with a rotating schedule, along with counseling by those who were knowledgeable, virtually everyone took turns participating.

I clearly remember several details in regard to food preparation that were related over the years. Food was generally divided by twosomes. One man prepared and separated what food there was—as equally as possible. The other would then pick which of the two portions he would choose to eat. Also, Harlan was a stickler when it came to peeling the skin off of potatoes. He constantly volunteered to do the peeling, since he felt that other POWs did not peel the skin thin enough. He did not want any edible potato to go to waste.

The following are Harlan's remarks about life in general while a prisoner:

P.O.W. time:

> *Not enough to eat—big guys lost 30-40 pounds in first month*
>
> *Usually cold in Germany*
>
> *Lots of roll-calls, lock-outs, and searches*
>
> *Lots of boredom, short tempers— a few broke under the constant fear Germany could not feed us, and thus would cut down on the number*
>
> *Read a lot, slept a lot, played a lot of bridge and poker (poker on I.O.U.s). One guy $5,000 in hole—I collected about $500 and paid out a little over $200* [after the war]

On the home front, things were undoubtedly difficult. The weeks and months of uncertainty had to weigh heavily on Beulah, who continued to teach at Richardson Park and live at home with her parents.

One bright spot for her occurred on September 29, 1944. In a ceremony at the New Castle Army Air Base (later, Wilmington Airport), Beulah was presented with Harlan's Air Medal. That military decoration was established in May 1942, and was awarded retroactively to September 1939. Although there has been varying specific criteria, generally the Air Medal is awarded to anyone who distinguishes himself or herself by meritorious achievement while participating in aerial flight. I feel sure it is safe to say that both Harlan and Beulah would have willingly traded the medal and the recognition to be back together instead.

On October 21, 1944, which was six days after his one-year anniversary in Stalag Luft III, Harlan turned twenty-nine.

1945

By January 1945, Allied forces were closing in on Germany from three directions. From the south, the Allies pushed upward through Italy; from the west, The Battle of the Bulge would be a hard-earned Allied victory; and from the east, Russian forces advanced relentlessly.

With the threat of an evacuation march occurring within a short period of time, on January 23 a directive was posted by the American Camp Staff of Stalag Luft III. It stated that all prisoners were to walk ten laps around the perimeter of the camp each day. This distance totaled seven and a half miles. To enhance the physical preparation, some POWs carried makeshift packs to simulate actual marching conditions.

Four days later on January 27, and with the Russian military within a range of 15 to 30 miles of Stalag Luft III, Hitler ordered an evacuation of the camp. He was fearful that the 10,000 Allied airmen would be liberated by the Russians, and he wanted to keep them as hostages.

Late in the evening, the POWs were given less than an hour's notice to gather all of their belongings for a withdrawal march. There was a scurry of activity that followed. In general, the POWs were ill-prepared from a clothing stand-point to endure the outdoor elements—near-or-below zero temperatures with wind-whipped snow falling.

Around midnight, all prisoners were lined up outside the camp's entrance and were counted. After a two-hour wait, and with six inches of snow already on the ground, German guards with sentinel dogs began herding some 10,000 Kriegies on a westward 60-mile forced march. It became famously known as The Long March. Hundreds of POWs died along the way from malnutrition, exhaustion, exposure, or a combination of all three.

The POWs marched single file in a line that stretched for miles. During the initial 11 hours, the prisoners advanced southwestward 18 miles to the town of Freiwaldau. The march was only interrupted by occasional ten-minute rest periods with no shelter from the driving snowstorm.

At Freiwaldau, the buildings of a former concentration camp provided temporary shelter. But because of the inadequate size of the buildings, the prisoners were shuttled through in two-hour shifts to warm up, while those arriving before and after waited outside in the blizzard.

There was intermittent shelter over the next several days in large factory buildings and churches, during which the driving snow and bitter temperatures continued. After a two-day break, the march resumed in moderating temperatures, but melting sheet ice on the roads made for continued uncomfortable walking conditions.

Harlan's brief notes regarding the march:

Russians got close, marched us out in snow storm—only 60 miles but kinda rough—6 or 7 days

When the POWs finally arrived at Spremberg, Germany, they were crammed into boxcars, which had been recently used for transporting livestock. Each of these French-made boxcars was known as a "forty-and-eight." The numbers referred to the normal capacity of either 40 men or 8 horses. Significantly smaller in size than standard American boxcars, these cars measured only slightly over 20 feet long and 8 feet wide. With 60 prisoners loaded into each boxcar that might have generally held 40, it created extremely overcrowded conditions.

Harlan notes: *About 60 in a car—took turns sitting down to sleep*

The southbound 200+ mile ordeal lasted three days and became increasingly foul with the stench of vomit and excrement. The only ventilation in the cars came from two small windows near the ceiling on opposite ends of the cars.

Harlan's notes indicate there was a stop near Nuremberg, Germany prior to reaching the eventual destination of Stalag VII-A, which had been Harlan's first German camp. Based on further research, it is apparent that some POWs were dropped off at Stalag XIII-D near Nuremberg.

During the overall course of the trip, the Allied commanding officer passed the word authorizing escape attempts. Roughly 32 men felt physically able to make the try. But in 36 hours, all had been recaptured. Harlan did not participate in these escape efforts.

When the remaining group, of which Harlan was a member, arrived at Stalag VII-A, conditions were a complete disaster. The camp was originally built to hold about 14,000 prisoners. At this point, approximately 110,000 POWs were massively overflowing the capacity. Some barracks were empty shells with dirt floors. In others, bunks were strapped together in blocks of 12 in an attempt to hold 500 prisoners per barrack—when 200 would have been cramped. All of the buildings were infested with vermin. Some POWs even moved out of the barracks and into tents that were erected to hold the increasing number of incoming prisoners who had been evacuated from other stalags.

Two months later, the ultimate insult occurred for those POWs who were previously unloaded at Stalag XIII-D. They were forced to march the ninety-mile distance south to VII-A.

Harlan's notes state: *Last 3 months in a real hell-hole—little food—lots of bedbugs—no bath—pneumonia*

The liberation of Stalag VII-A happened practically by accident. On April 28, 1945, the 14th Armored Division, which was part of the 7th Army commanded by General George S. Patton, had advanced southeastward for 50 miles against sporadic resistance. They had reached within four miles of Moosburg, the location of Stalag VII-A.

During the early morning hours of Sunday, April 29, German forces offered an armistice for the entire area surrounding Moosburg. One of the conditions cited in the German proposal was to delay the disposition of a significant number of Allied prisoners held in the vicinity. Up until this point, the commanders of the 14th Armored Division had not even known that there was a prison camp at Moosburg, much less how large it was. The negotiations included an approximate location of the camp.

The proposal was rejected by the Allies, and shortly thereafter a portion of the 14th advanced toward Moosburg. A hasty, uneven battle followed between American tanks and retreating German solders for control of bridges over the nearby Amper and Isar Rivers. The German forces had no tanks or anti-tank guns, and were equipped with only small arms and mortars.

Throughout the morning, there were ripples of excitement within Stalag VII-A as Allied artillery rocked the countryside. It was apparent to the POWs that liberation was in reach. As machine gun and rifle rounds zipped through parts of the camp, many prisoners laid low in safety. And although some long-range rounds briefly landed inside the camp, in general, Allied artillery was not used in the liberation for fear of injuring the prisoners.

Early in the afternoon, German resistance came to an end. The first of Patton's tanks entered the camp by rumbling through the double barbed wire fence. More tanks followed and the entire camp went into an unrestrained uproar. There were hugs and there were tears. So many POWs climbed onto the liberating tanks that they practically disappeared from sight. The Nazi flag was taken down and an American flag was run up the flagpole. There was joyous pandemonium.

Research has produced conflicting reports, but either later the same day or within several days, General Patton triumphantly entered the camp to another round of jubilant celebration. Tens of thousands of POWs were liberated at last!

Because of freeing Stalag VII-A, and other prison camps that followed, the 14th Armored Division took on the nickname, "Liberators."

Although my father left no notes regarding the liberation, I do recall him briefly referring to the event with a comment such as, *"Patton's tanks rolled in and liberated us."* This would always be followed by a smile.

Meanwhile, Russian forces advanced to close proximity of Berlin, hundreds of miles to the north. Although there were many areas of Germany still controlled by the Nazis, the following day, on April 30, Hitler and his wife of one day, Eva Braun, committed suicide in Hitler's "Fuhrerbunker." And only eight days thereafter, on May 8, the Germans unconditionally surrendered to Allied forces on what would become known as VE Day (Victory in Europe).

After the liberation, what followed in Stalag VII-A was a period of frustration and disappointment. The German guards were collected as prisoners and carted off. Also, advancing Allied forces had no capability to adequately administer to the needs of the sheer number of liberated POWs. There was a major delay until a U.S. Army support battalion arrived to handle the operation of the camp.

The first group of POWs to leave Stalag VII-A were French prisoners. Gen. Dwight D. Eisenhower had given French General Charles de Gaulle first priority for their transport. Against orders, many anxious American prisoners quietly left the camp and hitched rides to Paris.

Eventually, all remaining Americans were transported to nearby German airfields and flown by C-47 aircraft to the port city of Le Havre, France. From there the former POWs boarded what was known as a "Victory Ship" or "Liberty Ship" for the short trip across the English Channel to Southampton, England. From liberation until reaching England entailed a period of approximately two weeks.

It was during this time that several articles appeared in the Wilmington newspaper regarding the liberation of Delaware POWs. The first stated:

Four More Delaware Men
Freed From Prison Camps

"…Lieut. Highfield, who was reported missing in action in North Africa on March 29, 1943 and later a prisoner of the Germans, has been liberated according to word received by his wife Mrs. Beulah Papperman Highfield, 606 West Twenty-third Street, from the Red Cross last night.

And on May 15, 1945, along with a photograph:

Service Men Liberated by Allies
…Former School Teacher

"Lieutenant Highfield was interned in a prison camp near Munich. His wife received his Air Medal on Sept. 29, 1944 at ceremonies at the New Castle Army Air Base.

He is the son of Mr. and Mrs. Clarence J. Highfield of Bear. The flier was teaching at Richardson Park School when he entered the Army Air Forces in December 1941. He received his wings and commission at Spence Field, Moultrie, Ga."

Service Men Liberated by Allies

Lieut. Harlan E. Highfield

Lieut. Highfield, who was reported missing in action in North Africa on March 29, 1943 and later a prisoner of the Germans, has been liberated according to word received by his wife Mrs. Beulah Papperman Highfield, 606 West Twenty-third Street, from the Red Cross last night.

Former School Teacher

Lieutenant Highfield was interned in a prison camp near Munich. His wife received his Air Medal on Sept. 29, 1944 at ceremonies at the New Castle Army Air Base.

He is the son of Mr. and Mrs. Clarence J. Highfield of Bear. The flier was teaching at the Richardson Park School when he entered the Army Air Forces in December 1941. He received his wings and commission at Spence Field, Moultrie, Ga.

For the return voyage to the United States, nearly a hundred freighters and tankers provided transport across the Atlantic Ocean for thousands of servicemen. The ship that Harlan was aboard departed England on May 24, 1945 and arrived at New York City ten days later on June 3. What an emotional experience it must have been to reach New York Harbor and see the Statue of Liberty standing as a welcoming symbol of freedom.

I remember the story of my father's return to Wilmington being told many times over by my mother. It went something like this: Upon his arrival at the Wilmington Train Station, my father called my mother at her parents' house. He told her that he was home and that he had grown a mustache. He wanted to know if he should leave it on or if he should shave. Her quick reply was, "Shave it off." My parents always laughed heartily about that conversation.

After a cab ride from the train station to the intersection of Baynard Boulevard and West 23rd Street, my father walked the short distance around the corner to his in-law's house where my mother was waiting on the front porch. She always said later that seeing him walking toward the house was a vision she would never forget. They were finally reunited after a very long two years and nine months apart.

Later that summer, a reunion for return-ing war veterans and POWs was held in Atlantic

City, New Jersey. My parents attended, and on August 15 they were walking on the famed boardwalk when word spread like wildfire that the Japanese had surrendered. It would become known as VJ Day (Victory over Japan). The war was now ended on both sides of the globe.

My mother often told the story of the reaction of the jubilant crowd that packed the boardwalk. Hugging, kissing, tears of joy, and all-out bedlam reigned. It was a celebration like that of a New Year's Eve—multiplied a hundred times over. She would usually finish the story with a self-conscious giggle. Because of her traditionalist upbringing, I think she may have felt embarrassed by such openly raucous behavior.

A negative point my father made regarding that reunion event, and others like it, was the overindulgence of food by former POWs. At every turn, plentiful buffets were readily available. As he would dejectedly describe the re-acclamation of ex-prisoners to a regular diet: *"Some guys ate themselves to death."* Whenever I heard him make that statement I could tell he meant it in a literal sense. POWs had been denied adequate nutrition and sufficient intake of food to the extent that they could not control their consumption when it was again commonly accessible.

As the summer ended, he notes, *"Beulie and I were finally ready to start our lives together."*

Tapestry embroidered by Harlan's mother,
Emily B. Highfield

After the War

Harlan received the following decorations as a result of his service during World War II:

Air Medal -- Purple Heart -- Distinguished Unit Badge -- European-African-Middle Eastern Theatre Ribbon with one Battle Star -- Prisoner of War Medal -- World War II Medal

Of these decorations, I believe he was most honored by the Prisoner of War Medal. In later life, my father was grateful for the license plate for his car that was issued from the State of Delaware, which reads: EX POW. I am in possession of the above medals and the com-memorative license plate.

In referring to the length of time he was captive, my mother was always very specific in saying it had been "twenty-five months." And, in fact, it was exactly twenty-five months to the day: March 29, 1943 to April 29, 1945. It is peculiar that the dates came out to such a precise number, but it must have seemed much longer to both of them.

My father had lingering issues for the rest of his life as a result of the wounds he received. On a later Former POW Medical History form he completed for the Veterans Administration, the following responses are some that appear:

Describe your injury(ies): machine gun wound of left triceps and right femur.

Did you participate in a plan to escape: Yes

Did you make an active attempt to escape: Yes

If so, were you successful: No

Isolation in close quarters – Hospital ship: Yes

Railroad Cars: Yes

If you were held in a railroad car, was it attacked: Yes

Solitary confinement: No

Forced marches: Yes

Describe your worst experiences as a captive: (a) "Round-Up" for a few hours where we felt we might be

destroyed to relieve transport problem
(b) In boxcar near Switzerland while
the marshalling yard was being bombed

<u>Did the VA give you a disability rating</u>
<u>after repatriation:</u> Yes

<u>If yes, what was the percentage:</u> 50+

<u>What was the disability:</u> Loss of
efficiency of right leg and left arm

<u>Despite the many negative aspects</u>
<u>of your POW status, were there any</u>
<u>positive aspects to your experience:</u> I
learned to place less importance on
material things, than I had before

     I can attest to several enduring effects from
the war that my father carried with him. Despite
having sustained a .50 caliber bullet wound of
his right femur, I cannot recall him walking with
a noticeable limp in his stride. However, if he
were to stand for an extended time, especially on
a hard surface such as tile or concrete, he would
show signs of discomfort.

     To a much greater extent, if he hit the end
of the middle finger of his left hand on a hard
surface, it would send him into a brief period
of intense agony. Losing a portion of his triceps
affected the nerves in his left arm, and the damage

manifested itself in that particular finger. My description of his reaction is no exaggeration. I witnessed it many times growing up when we had a catch with a baseball. Being right-handed, he wore his glove on his left hand. And although he took great effort to pad his finger and glove, it seemed almost inevitable the catch would end abruptly and painfully for him. This was especially true as I got older and could throw the ball harder. That reality made it a bittersweet experience for both of us. But he was virtually always the one to suggest having the catch each time.

Although the term Posttraumatic Stress Disorder (PTSD) was not used until more recent years, I believe my father suffered from it. A loud or startling noise would always cause a jumpy response from him. I think the trauma he experienced in a boxcar during the bombing of the train depot near Switzerland was the culprit for that type of reaction. The explosions and concussions in close proximity, while in a confined space, had to leave a strong impression.

In spite of the various lingering issues my father dealt with, he never displayed any outward signs of lament or negativism about them. It was always life as usual on his part.

A positive development coming out of WWII were the lasting friendships my father established with several fellow POWs. Two life-long buddies come to mind. Max Rickless (who was known as Rick) of New York was a bomber navigator whose plane had been shot down in Italy. A yearly exchange of seasonal greetings and letters went on for many years between Rick and his wife, Sylvia, and my parents.

Another close bond continued for over forty years with Tony Dold and his wife, Mary Rose, of South Africa. Tony had also been a fighter pilot who was shot down and became a POW. In addition to yearly Christmas cards, the Dolds traveled to the U.S. in the 1980s and visited with Beulah and Harlan. I can always remember my parents having upbeat and cheerful feelings for both of these couples.

When the new school year began in September of 1945, both of my parents returned to their regular spots on the faculty of the Richardson Park School. My mother had continued to teach third grade during the war. And my father went back to teaching seventh and eighth grade science as well as gym classes, along with coaching both basketball and baseball.

For their first home, they rented an apartment on the second floor of a bank building in Newport, Delaware, which was only several miles from the school. It was during this time that Harlan was promoted from 2nd to 1st Lieutenant. And on November 30, 1945, Harlan received official notification from the Army Air Corps that he was relieved of active duty. He would receive his Honorable Discharge from service on January 10, 1956.

At the end of my father's first year back teaching, on June 16, 1946, my brother, Gus (Harlan, Jr.), was born. An early addition to the Baby Boomer Generation!

Over the course of the next four years, there was much activity in the Highfield family. My father's teaching and coaching moved from Richardson Park to Warner Jr. High School in Wilmington. He also coached American Legion baseball during the summer, which was for older boys aged 15-17. That coaching culminated in the summer of 1950, when my father managed the Five Points Boys Club American Legion team to the Delaware State Championship. Just turning four, Gus was the team mascot. I came along in April 1950, but due to some early health issues, I wasn't available to cheer on the team that summer.

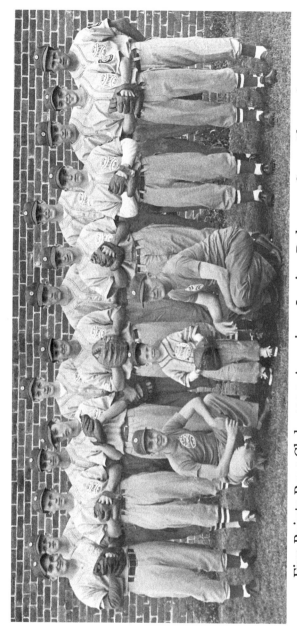

Five Points Boys Club, 1950 American Legion Delaware State Champions.
Mgr. Harlan Highfield, front left; Gus Highfield, age 4, front middle

With a desire for our family to own and live in a single-family home, during 1948-50 my father designed and built two houses. He contracted out much of the work. During construction, the first house became too expensive for his budget so he sold it upon completion. In more recent years, that former residence has housed a daycare and early learning center. The second house was finished around the time I was born, and we lived in it until I was eleven.

It wasn't all teaching and coaching on my father's part during the early 1950s. In summers and evenings, he embarked on graduate courses at the University of Delaware in pursuit of his Master's degree. Majoring in Child Guidance and Development, he was awarded his Master of Education in 1952.

The higher education didn't stop there. He continued taking courses at U. of D. for his "Plus 30" though 1956, majoring in Administration and Supervision. Combined, he earned a total of 66 graduate credits. With the coursework completed, he was accepted for Doctoral work at both Temple and Columbia Universities. However, as he put it, *"Scholarships were inadequate to meet my responsibilities."*

Honorable Discharge

from the Armed Forces of the United States of America

This is to certify that

FIRST LIEUTENANT HARLAN E. HIGHFIELD, AO 791 105, AIR FORCE RESERVE

was Honorably Discharged from the

United States Air Force

on the TENTH *day of* JANUARY 1956 *This certificate is awarded as a testimonial of Honest and Faithful Service*

JAMES T. QUIRK
Colonel, USAF

DD FORM 256 AF   PREVIOUS EDITIONS OF THIS FORM MAY BE USED.
1 NOV 51

His professional career continued on an upward plane also. From 1953 through 1957, he was Vice Principal of two different junior high schools in Wilmington, followed by a year as Assistant Principal of Wilmington High School. It was from that position he left Wilmington in 1958 for the smaller Stanton School District southwest of the city. The area was a growing suburb, and he was groomed to replace the retiring superintendent.

Serving as the District Superintendent from 1959 until his retirement in 1971, he oversaw the construction of four elementary schools, two junior high schools, as well as one special education school. Teaching and coaching were his passions, but he also was more than capable as an administrator.

During his career in (as he always put it) *"the school business,"* he was a member of seven education associations spanning national, state, and local levels. He was also a member of an honorary Educational Research fraternity. And in 1964 he was listed in the publication, "Who's Who in American Education."

In addition to these professional organizations, he was a Charter Member of the Kiwanis Club of Red Clay Valley where he served in various roles over the course of seven years. These included President, Secretary, Editor of the weekly bulletin, and Chairman of the Boys' and Girls' Work Committee. He also served on the Board of Directors of the Western Branch Y.M.C.A. for three years, and on the Board of Sanford Preparatory School for two years.

Community activities included several years with each of the following: P.T.A. Program Chairman, Cub Scouts Committeeman, Summer Playground Director, University of Delaware Scholarship Committeeman, Director of Dickinson High School Athletic Boosters, Advisor of a Senior Hi-Y Club, and President of the Linden Knoll Condominium Association.

In the year after his retirement from the school district, he served as Acting Manager of the newly-constructed Pike Creek Valley Country Club, which at the time was Delaware's most recent 18-hole championship golf course. His modest abilities as a golfer were finally rewarded with this management position!

Personal interests in his spare time over the years were stamp collecting and genealogy research. He also was an avid fan of the comic strip, "Peanuts." Snoopy was his favorite character whose droll sense of humor meshed with that of my father. He enjoyed making up invitations, brochures, and reports with images of Peanuts characters included. And a prized possession in later life was a retirement gift of a personally autographed drawing of Charlie Brown and Snoopy by their creator, Charles Schultz.

Above and beyond this extensive list of career achievements, memberships, and other activities, without a doubt my father's perpetual interest throughout his life was baseball. He continued coaching school baseball through 1954, after which he moved from teaching to administration. Having completed his graduate studies, a return to coaching in the summers occurred in 1957 when both my brother, Gus, and I were beginning to play Little League baseball.

Through his involvement with the Kiwanis Club, he was the driving force during 1959 in the construction of a baseball field on Newport-Gap Pike, south of Wilmington, which was named Kiwanis Field. The field has been in continuous use by the Little League ever since and is currently called Catalina Field.

Except for a one-year hiatus, he coached summer baseball through 1968. That year, he managed his second American Legion Delaware State Championship team (Pike Creek Valley). I was a starting player on that team, which was undefeated during the regular season.

Pike Creek Valley, 1968 American Legion Delaware State Champions.
Mgr. Harlan Highfield, standing 3rd from left; Chuck Highfield, kneeling 2nd from left

Jumping back into baseball in 1977, he was the head coach of a team (Marta Construction) in the Delaware Semi-Pro League, which was runner-up in the league playoffs. I also played on that team.

A rewarding summer for both of us occurred in 1980 when we worked together coaching a team in the Millcreek Babe Ruth League. We went on to also coach the league All-Star team.

Throughout the course of coaching baseball at all levels (school and summer) during a total of 27 seasons, he compiled an overall record of 283 wins and 106 losses, for a .728 winning percentage.

Closing Thoughts

My father certainly was a busy man throughout his life, both before and after World War II. It is only speculation on my part that after the setback of having to repeat the 12th grade in high school, and then later his commitment of three and a half years in the Army Air Corps (25 months captive), he lived his life in a continual effort to make up for lost time.

That concept was demonstrated in a heartfelt letter his father wrote to him during the later stages of the war while my father was still a POW. Although the letter dealt with other issues of their relationship over the years, it contained the following line: "I hope when this war is over that the life you lead will make up for all you lost."

The most ironic feature of my father's remarkable drive and determination is that there were times when he would refer to himself as being lazy. If he took a nap (a "snooze" as he called it) or if he "loafed" for a short period, I think he felt somewhat guilty for losing productive time. And yet, it seemed to me that he was always either doing something—or thinking about, and planning out, the next thing he wanted to do. He indeed packed a lot into his life.

One of his fundamental beliefs was that principles and ethics ought to be followed. One of these that I recall him impressing upon me was when, in his mind, negative behavior is observed, it should be pointed out. He believed by not doing that, one was complying with such behavior. That approach would occasionally elicit less-than-cordial responses.

My father was always one for using expressions. He loved to say, *"Baseball is a game of inches."* In retrospect, I suppose it could be said that war is, also. The .50 caliber bullets that wounded him were inches away from certain death.

In terms of playing sports to win, he liked, *"If winning wasn't important, they wouldn't keep score."*

Another expression he used was, *"Why practice anything you have to do perfectly the first time?"* That one may possibly be attributed to the successful crash landing of his P-40 in the Tunisian desert. He surely was only getting one chance to make it to the ground safely.

Thirty-six years would pass before he set foot on an airplane again. In 1979, my parents went with friends on a two-week vacation to England. During the flight to London, their companions passed word to the crew regarding my father's WWII background. The pilot of the plane invited him to the flight deck for a visit.

I remember it being said later that he was over-whelmed with the numerous instruments and gauges. The technology he recalled of the P-40 had been vastly improved—and complicated.

He gained an expression in his first stint in American Legion baseball from Ralph Dill, who coached with him. As Mr. Dill put it, "We don't need to teach these boys how to be boys; they already know that. We need to teach them how to be men." And although he never claimed it as his own, I believe my father carried that one with him for the rest of his life.

While winning was a strong motivation in his coaching career, at its core was a desire to develop character in his players. Over the years, his successful pursuit of that goal has been repeatedly evidenced by comments from former players. Many times, they have spoken highly of the positive impact he had on them, and how he imparted not just baseball skills, but life skills.

The lengthy period in captivity my father endured was, without a doubt, difficult. A motivating factor throughout was his desire to return home to his bride, whom he had been with only a mere month after their wedding. Being liberated from the prison camp was a metaphor for being free to return home and begin their lives together. And, by the way, Gus and I are forever grateful his homecoming came to be.

As was his occasional custom, his notes also contain several satirical comments, which were aimed at the Army Air Corps. In regard to how the schedule changed in the early going from what he was told, and what actually happened, he writes,

[Was] *promised not* [to] *go overseas before first of year, so got married* [in August]. *So left for Africa via Puerto Rico in October* [the month of my] *birthday*....

World War II was a devastating experience for all. Many lives were taken and many lives were changed forever. It is highly understandable that veterans of the conflict almost universally set the subject away from their consciousness. Even though they remembered that awful period and their lives prior, it was as if a line was drawn when the war ended. A time to start over had begun.

There are those who have portrayed my father as a hero. He would have none of that. He looked at the war the same way he looked at coaching a team. The concept of working together to accomplish an objective through teamwork was always the idea. It seems likely this was the consensus feeling of many who fought in World War II. There is a certain selflessness in that sentiment, and I know my father believed it and practiced it to the highest degree. It was never about individuals;

it was continually about what was best for everyone.

In response to that "hero" talk, he would no doubt deflect it to include the many others who also endured the agonizing hostilities—at any and all levels. He would simply say something like,

Things were rough all over...

Acknowledgements

To *Gayle Kasey*, for editorial assistance, suggestions, and creative ideas

To *Gus Highfield*, for editorial assistance and valued recommendations

To *Captain Wes Turner*, for knowledge of the aviation industry

To *Thomas Urech*, for language translation

To *Bayard R. Horn*, former P.O.W. and Purple Heart recipient, for his remembrances of World War II

A NOTE ABOUT THE AUTHOR

A native of Delaware, W. C. (Chuck) Highfield graduated from the University of Delaware in 1972. He has always been an avid participant in sports. Highfield's baseball career culminated with playing ten years in the Delaware Semi-Pro League. Later, he took up running and participated in numerous road races.

Highfield has written three novels, all of which are set in Florida. Each story explores the diverse range of human behavior.

With **LIBERATED, A World War II Memoir of Lt. Harlan E. Highfield**, he has changed course entirely. The author presents a factual timeline of his father's World War II experiences. Highfield blends historical research, as well as his personal remembrances, with his father's extensive records.

Since 2006, Chuck Highfield resides and writes in Fort Myers, Florida.

Novels by the Author

IN SUN DOWN FAR

STREETS

SANIBEL'S SECRET BANK

www.WCHighfield.com